BIG PICTURE PRESS

First published in the UK in 2016 by Big Picture Press,
an imprint of Kings Road Publishing,
part of the Bonnier Publishing Group,
The Plaza, 535 King's Road, London, SW10 0SZ
www.bonnierpublishing.com

First published by Penguin Random House
Australia Pty Ltd, 2016

ISBN 978-1-78370-465-1

Cover and text design by Marc Martin and Bruno Herfst
©Penguin Random House Australia, 2016
Colour separation by Splitting Image Colour Studio,
Clayton, Victoria

Printed in Malaysia

LOTS

by Marc Martin

BPP

YOU ARE HERE

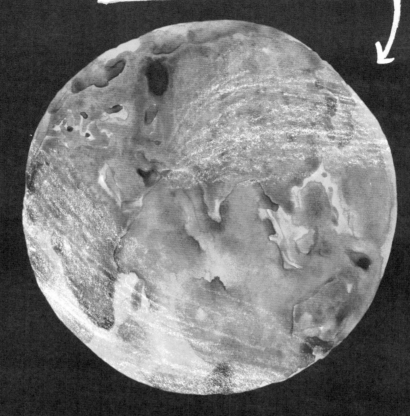

...or maybe you're here?

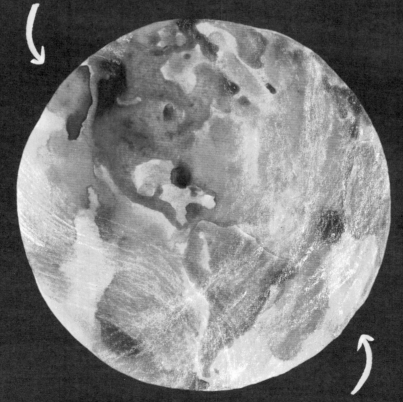

Maybe one day you'll go here

A NOTE FROM THE AUTHOR

How many cats live in Cairo? How much cheese does a Parisian eat each day? What is Pylsusinnep? These are just some of the many questions you might ask about the world we live in.

The following pages are a gathering of facts, thoughts and observations about our planet. Some may intrigue you, some may surprise you, and some may leave you with more questions than answers.

From cities to forests and deserts to oceans, there's so much to discover. All you need is a good guide and a little curiosity...

So, what are you waiting for? Let's start exploring!

ANTARCTICA

The coldest and windiest continent on Earth. Bring a good jacket!

Southern Right whale

WHALES
Feed in the nutrient-rich Southern Ocean

Minke whale

Human size compared to whale size

Finback whale

Sperm whale

Blue whale
Weighs 190,000kg

Killer whale (Orca)

Humpback whale

PENGUINS
20 million breeding pairs of penguins

Adélie penguin

ATMs
One place to get money on the whole continent (McMurdo Station)

Gentoo penguin

Emperor penguin

Chinstrap penguin

ROSS ICE SHELF ← 800 km across →

ICEBERGS
Of all shapes and sizes

RESEARCH STATIONS
From all around the world

Bharati Station (India)

SANAE IV (South Africa)

Princess Elisabeth Station (Belgium)

Neumayer Station III (Germany)

Jang Bogo Station (South Korea)

Taishan Station (China)

Halley VI Station (United Kingdom)

Amundsen-Scott Station (United States)

Concordia (France/Italy)

ICE BREAKERS
Used to clear a path for other boats

SNOW PETRELS
Breed exclusively in Antarctica

SHIPPING CONTAINERS
Used to transport supplies

WIND
Up to 320km/h

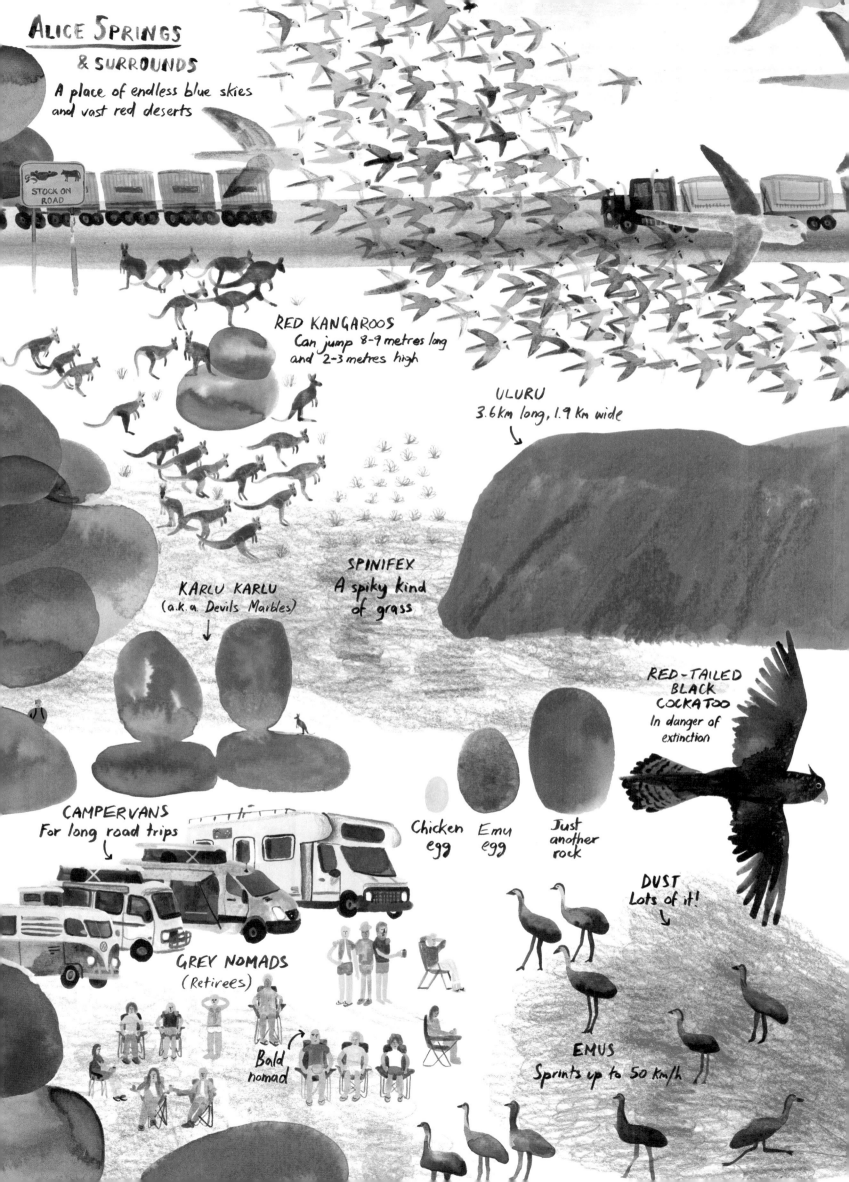

ALICE SPRINGS
& SURROUNDS
A place of endless blue skies and vast red deserts

STOCK ON ROAD

RED KANGAROOS
Can jump 8-9 metres long and 2-3 metres high

ULURU
3.6km long, 1.9 km wide

KARLU KARLU
(a.k.a. Devils Marbles)

SPINIFEX
A spiky kind of grass

RED-TAILED BLACK COCKATOO
In danger of extinction

CAMPERVANS
For long road trips

Chicken egg   Emu egg   Just another rock

DUST
Lots of it!

GREY NOMADS
(Retirees)

Bald nomad

EMUS
Sprints up to 50 km/h

BLUE SKIES
As far as the eye can see

ROAD TRAINS
Long trucks with many trailers

WIND MILLS
For pumping water

ROAD TRAINS
53 METRES LONG

← Long straight roads →

DINGOES
The largest terrestrial predators in Australia

BUDGERIGARS
Fly in large flocks, and are very noisy!

MAJOR MITCHELL'S COCKATOO

Bad hair day

OPAL
Found in the mining town of Coober Pedy

COOBER PEDY

ROAD SIGNS
For every occasion

ROAD WARNING SIGNS ARE FOR YOUR PROTECTION PLEASE DON'T USE THEM FOR TARGETS

NEXT 96 km

GALAHS
Also known as rose-breasted cockatoos

Australian Aboriginal Flag

HONG KONG

Bustling streets, crowded skylines and one of the world's most densely populated metropolises

MARKETS AND SHOPPING

Sneakers street

Computer market

Jade market

Costume market

Goldfish market

Flower market

FRAGRANT HARBOUR
Hong Kong translates to 'fragrant harbour' in Chinese!

Business card market

FERRIES
135,000 passengers a day going to over 260 outlying islands

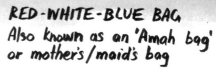

A SYMPHONY OF LIGHTS
The world's largest permanent light and sound show

RED-WHITE-BLUE BAG
Also known as an 'Amah bag' or mother's/maid's bag

SIGNS
Everywhere!

AIR CONDITIONERS
So humid!

Duddell Street
Hong Kong's
only gas lamps

20 minutes
from top to
bottom

Central-Mid-Levels
escalator (the longest
outdoor escalator
in the world)

Ladder
Street

STAIRS AND
ESCALATORS
For all those hills

DOUBLE-DECKER TRAMS
The world's largest fleet of
double-decker trams

EXPENSIVE
CARS
More Rolls-Royces
per person than
any other city

DIM SUM
Small bite-sized portions of food

- Beef tripe
- Chicken buns
- Pork buns
- Custard buns
- Chicken claws
- Custard roll
  sponge cake
- Pork and shrimp
  bean curd roll

BUBBLE TEA
Frothy tea
mixed with
tapioca balls

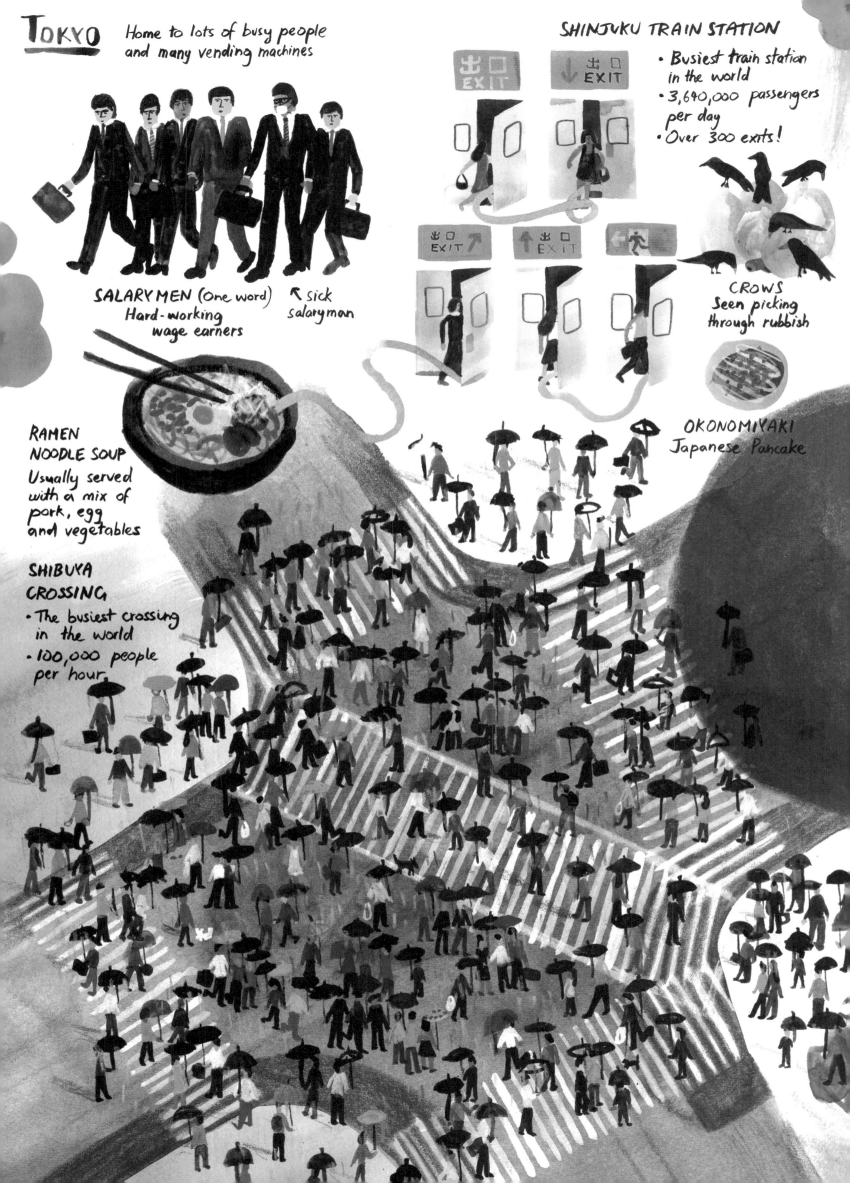

TOKYO
Home to lots of busy people and many vending machines

SHINJUKU TRAIN STATION
- Busiest train station in the world
- 3,640,000 passengers per day
- Over 300 exits!

SALARY MEN (One word)
Hard-working wage earners

↑ Sick salaryman

CROWS
Seen picking through rubbish

RAMEN NOODLE SOUP
Usually served with a mix of pork, egg and vegetables

OKONOMIYAKI
Japanese Pancake

SHIBUYA CROSSING
- The busiest crossing in the world
- 100,000 people per hour

VENDING MACHINES 5.6 million vending machines in Japan!

Flowers · Umbrellas · Books · Beer · Ramen · Fish bait · Tap beer · Wrong exit! · Soft drink · Beer

出口 EXIT

Bananas · Beer · Underwear · Neck ties · Milk · Coffee · More beer · Salad · Eggs

ONSEN
Japanese bath house

SHINKANSEN FAST TRAIN
Travels at 320 km/h

GODZILLA
Official citizen of Japan and has very bad breath

Sushi train

KAWAII
Cute things

CONVENIENCE STORES
On nearly every corner

出口 EXIT

Lobster vending machine

Cute toast · Cute potato · Cute cat · Cute cloud · Cute rice

CHERRY BLOSSOMS
Enjoy Hanami (flower viewing) in March/April

CICADAS
The sound of summer in Tokyo

ULAANBAATAR

Capital of Mongolia - one of the least densely populated countries in the world

Genghis Khan vodka

GENGHIS KHAN (c1162-1227)
a.k.a. Chinggis khaan Emperor of the Mongol Empire and featured on anything and everything

Genghis khan Equestrian Statue

Genghis Khan hotel

CHINGGIS KHAAN

Genghis Khan airport

40 metres high

Genghis Khan money

CHINGGIS KHAN

Genghis Khan cigarettes

MONGOLIAN FOOD

Süütei tsai Salty tea

Airag Fermented mare's milk

Guriltai Shul Noodle soup

Aaruul Dried milk curd

Buuz Steamed mutton dumplings

Khuushuur Deep fried dumplings

GERS
Portable round tents where many Mongolians live

NAADAM
A traditional festival consisting of wrestling, archery and horse racing

← FURGON VAN
Officially seats nine but usually fits as many as possible

BACTRIAN CAMELS
Two humps!

OVOOS
Sacred cairn made from rocks and wood. Circle three times clockwise for a safer journey while travelling

MONGOLIAN HORSE
Short, stocky breed native to Mongolia

YAKS
Used for thick shaggy fur and very tasty milk

GOBI DESERT
Approximately 1,295,000 km² and Asia's largest desert

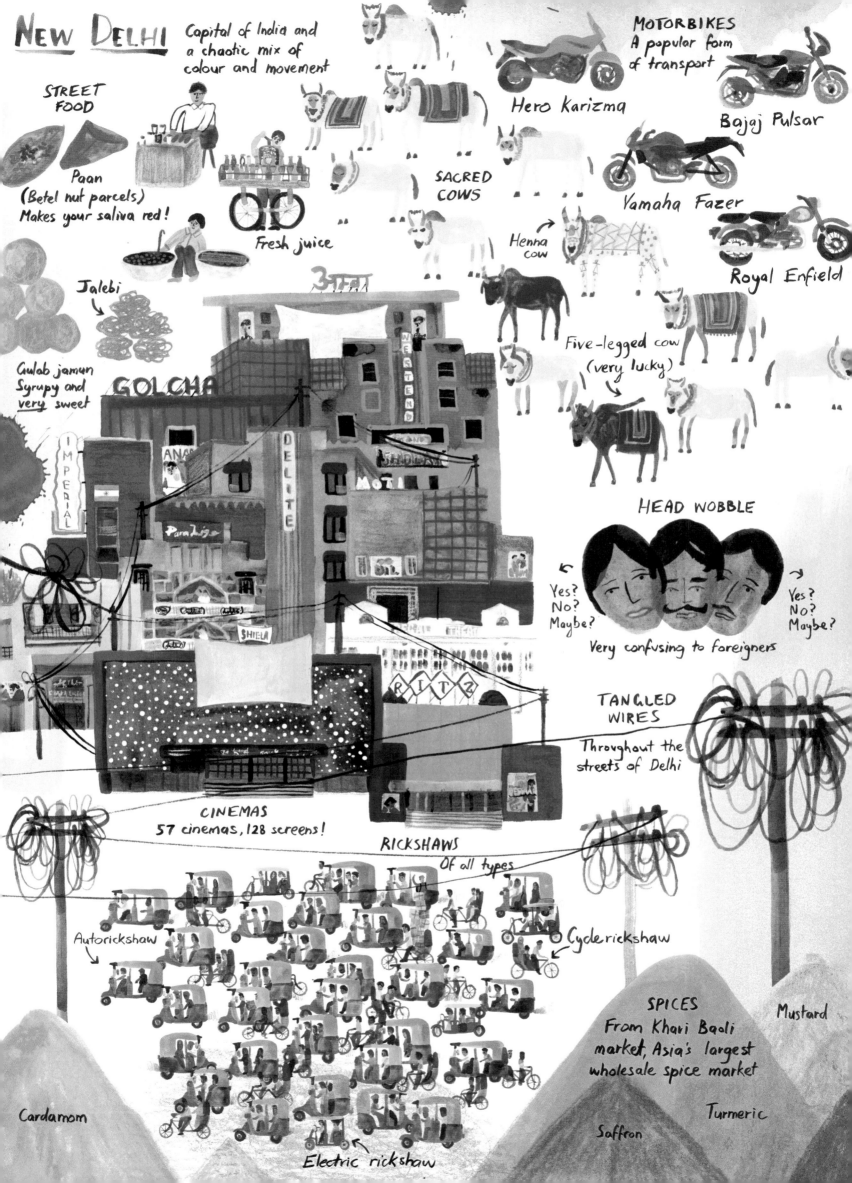

MANY MOUSTACHES In all shapes and lengths

BUSES World's largest fleet of environmentally friendly gas-powered buses

BANGLES In many colours

CHAI WALLAHS Make a great cup of tea

HENNA Used for decoration in ceremonies and special events

WEDDINGS Especially during wedding season (late Sept–Jan)

CHAI CUPS Made of clay. Break after drinking

GODS & DEITIES A small selection...

Saraswati

Lakshmi

Brahma

Ganesha

Vishnu

Parvati

CHILLI FOR MOTHER-IN-LAW (HOT!)

Shiva

Cumin

Fennel

Chilli

Nutmeg

Leningradskaya Hotel

Hotel Ukraina

Kudrinskaya Square Building

Red Gates Administrative Building

MATRYOSHKA DOLLS
A traditional Russian toy
(not to scale!)

POLICE OFFICERS
Around 50,000 of them

STRAY DOGS
An estimated 35,000 stray dogs, with some
known to ride the trains for food

PARK POBEDY METRO
The longest escalators
in Europe

126 metres
740 steps

← Yuri Gagarin
Cosmonaut and
the first human
in outer space

METRO
STATIONS
Palatial and
practical!

Kiyevskaya

Mayakovskaya

Elektrozavodskaya

Taganskaya

Komsomolskaya

9 million passengers per day

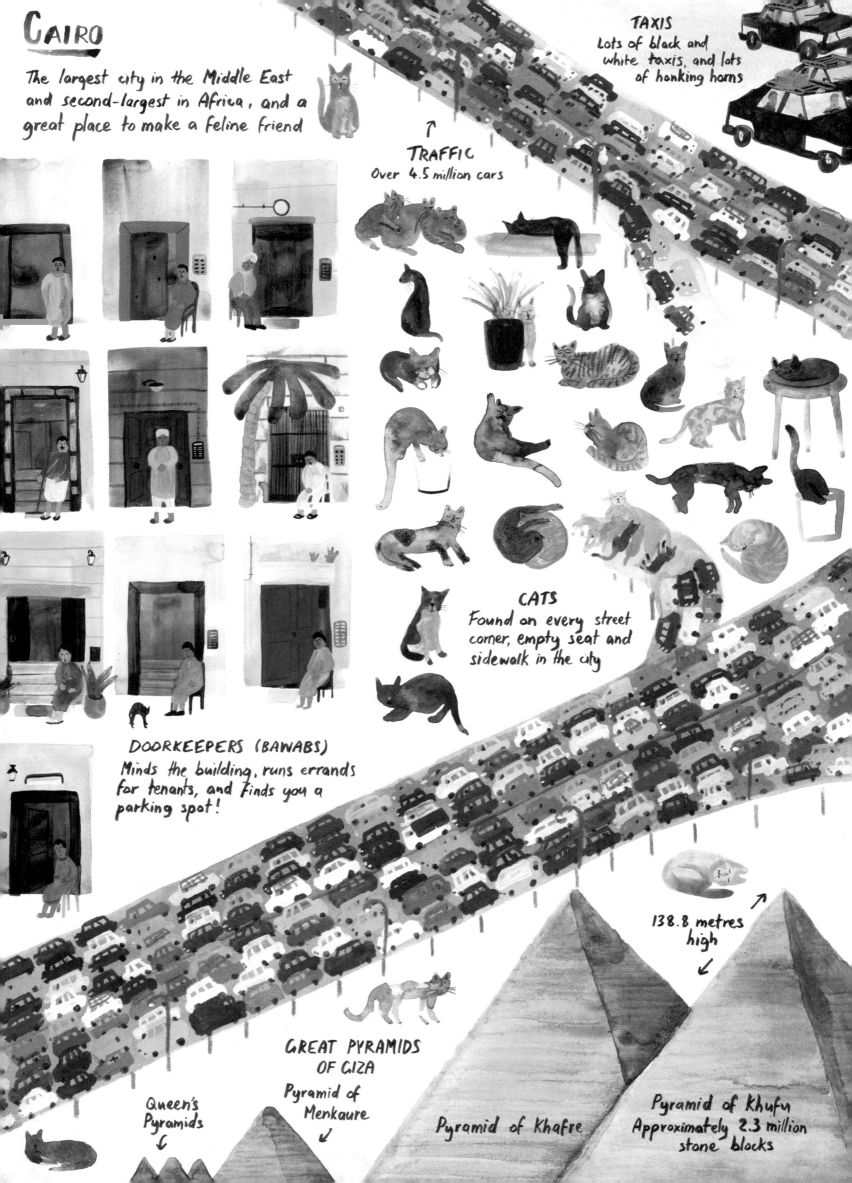

CAIRO

The largest city in the Middle East and second-largest in Africa, and a great place to make a feline friend

TAXIS
Lots of black and white taxis, and lots of honking horns

TRAFFIC
Over 4.5 million cars

CATS
Found on every street corner, empty seat and sidewalk in the city

DOORKEEPERS (BAWABS)
Minds the building, runs errands for tenants, and finds you a parking spot!

138.8 metres high

GREAT PYRAMIDS OF GIZA

Queen's Pyramids

Pyramid of Menkaure

Pyramid of Khafre

Pyramid of Khufu
Approximately 2.3 million stone blocks

KHAN EL-KHALILI BAZAAR
A major shopping district for antiques, jewellery and general goods

GOLD, BRASS AND SILVER GOODS

Plates

Jugs

Bowls

Lamps

EGYPTIAN FOOD

Fesikh
Fermented, salted and dried grey mullet

Fül
Cooked fava beans with oil, cumin, and parsley

Duqqa
A mixture of herbs, nuts and spices

Kushari
A mix of rice, macaroni and lentils

Mulukhiya
A soup made from finely chopped leaves from the Jute plant

Gibna Domiati
A soft salty cheese typically made from buffalo milk

Shisha on the go!

SHISHA PIPES AND SHISHA SMOKERS
A smoking pipe for flavoured tobacco and a very popular pastime

MINARETS
Cairo's nickname: 'The city of a thousand minarets'

 # PARIS

A cosmopolitan city, rich in art, food and culture

De l'art!

The Mona Lisa
(difficult to see)

THE LOUVRE MUSEUM
- Holds 70,000 pieces of art
- Employs 2000 staff
- Has 8.8 million visitors a year

CHEESE
Best served at room temperature

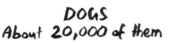

DOGS
About 20,000 of them

Camembert

Maroilles

Chèvre

Brie

 Beaufort

 Laguiole

Roquefort

 Valençay

 Comté

10 tons of dog droppings every day

Watch your step!

ROOFTOP APARTMENTS
Great views!

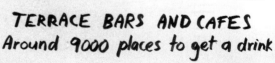

TERRACE BARS AND CAFES
Around 9000 places to get a drink

PHARMACIE

PHARMACIES
For all your health
and beauty needs

Pharmacy signs
everywhere

ARC DE TRIOMPHE
12 avenues radiating from the centre

WINE (VIN)
Common varieties:
- Bordeaux
- Champagne
- Pinot Noir
- Chardonnay
- Chenin • Merlot
- Grenache
- Malbec

BOULANGERIE
BOULANGERIE
Boulangerie Patisserie
BOULANGERIE · PATISSERIE
BOULANGERIE

BAKERIES Approximately 1800 bakeries

LE TOUR
DE FRANCE
- Up to 198 cyclists
- Approximately 3500 km
- 21 days long
- Always ends in Paris

Croissant

Pain au chocolat

Chausson
aux pommes

Pain aux
raisins

You can never
have too many
baguettes

Éclair

Flan   Mille-Feuille

Religieuse

Macarons

CAKES AND PASTRIES

Croissant aux
amandes

Not a
cake

Tarte
aux fraise

Opera

REYKJAVÍK

The capital of Iceland and home to many natural wonders ... and strange sauces

NAMES
The most common names in Iceland are Jón and Anna

Jón · Anna · Jón · Anna · Jón · Jón · Jón · Anna · Jón · Anna · Anna · Jón · Anna · Anna · Jón · Jón · Anna · Jón · Jón · Anna · Anna · Jón · Anna · Jón · Anna · Jón · Jón · Anna · Björk · Jón · Anna · Jón · Jón · Jón · Anna · Jón · Jón · Anna · Jón · Jón · Anna · Anna · Anna · Jón

The cairn formerly known as Jón

GEOTHERMAL POOLS
Very warm!

RE364

VOLCANOES
130 in Iceland

ARCTIC FOX
The only native mammal in Iceland

ATLANTIC PUFFINS
60% of the world's Atlantic puffins nest in Iceland

Baby puffin

ICELANDIC HORSE
Very photogenic

Anna

Jón

Jón

CAIRN
A pile of rocks used as a marker

CANS
Icelanders drink more cola per person than any other country

HOUSES
Many colourful rooftops

SAUCE

A sauce for everything!
- Hamborgarasósa
- Kokteilsósa
- Remoladi
- Pitusósa
- Grænmetissósa

PYLSUSINNEP
Mustard sauce

SKYR
A yoghurt/cheese-like food eaten for breakfast, as a snack or as a sauce

ARCTIC TERNS
Travel 71,000 km every year; the furthest migration route of any animal

FISHING BOATS

LIQUORICE
A popular treat

NORTHERN LIGHTS ↑
A spectacular lightshow caused by particles from the sun hitting the Earth's atmosphere

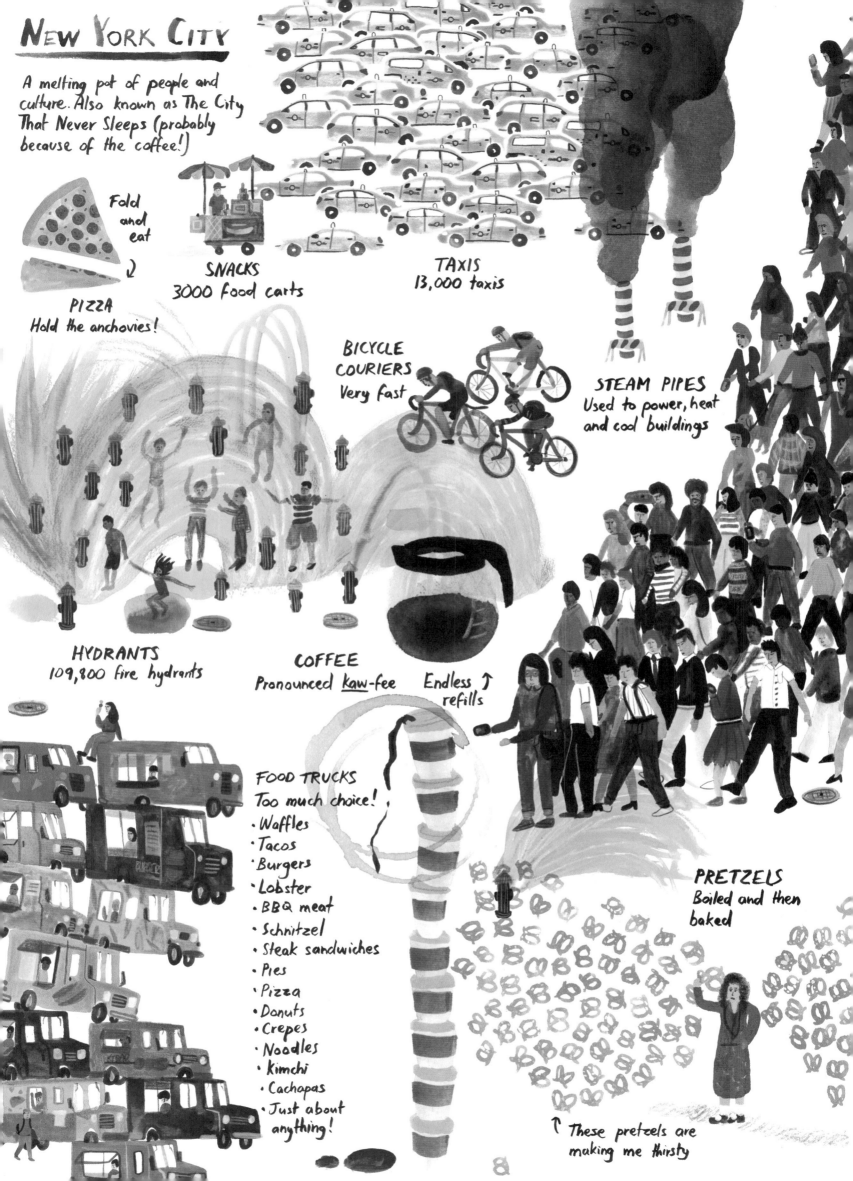

NEW YORK CITY

A melting pot of people and culture. Also known as The City That Never Sleeps (probably because of the coffee!)

PIZZA
Hold the anchovies!

Fold and eat ↓

SNACKS
3000 food carts

TAXIS
13,000 taxis

STEAM PIPES
Used to power, heat and cool buildings

BICYCLE COURIERS
Very fast

HYDRANTS
109,800 fire hydrants

COFFEE
Pronounced <u>kaw</u>-fee

Endless ↑ refills

FOOD TRUCKS
Too much choice!
- Waffles
- Tacos
- Burgers
- Lobster
- BBQ meat
- Schnitzel
- Steak sandwiches
- Pies
- Pizza
- Donuts
- Crepes
- Noodles
- Kimchi
- Cachapas
- Just about anything!

PRETZELS
Boiled and then baked

↑ These pretzels are making me thirsty

8

RATS
2 million rats

TIMES
SQUARE
Many lights
and signs

Tower
of Bagel

Not only
used by men!

CHRYSLER
BUILDING
3862 windows in
the Chrysler Building

MANHOLE COVERS
264,000 manhole covers

PEOPLE
8.5 million people from all
around the world, speaking
more than 800 languages

SKYSCRAPERS
Approximately 250
skyscrapers

BAGELS
Best served with
cream cheese

GALÁPAGOS ISLANDS

An archipelago of 19 islands inhabited by many unique and beautiful animals

LAVA CACTUS
Grows on lava fields

BLUE-FOOTED BOOBY (Bottom half)

LAVA LIZARDS
The most common reptiles on the island

Sharp-beaked ground finch

Not actually from the Galápagos, but still part of the group

Cocos Island finch

Cactus finch

DARWIN'S FINCHES
All linked by a common ancestor

Warbler finch

Large cactus finch

Mangrove finch

Large ground finch

MAGNIFICENT FRIGATEBIRD
Inflates its throat to attract a mate

Woodpecker finch

Medium ground finch

GIANT GALÁPAGOS TORTOISE
Can live to over 150 years old!

Small tree finch

Small ground finch

Medium tree finch

Vegetarian finch

Large tree finch

SCALESIA TREES
Endemic to the Galápagos

WAVED ALBATROSS
Partners for life

Isabela crece por ti

BLUE-FOOTED BOOBY (Top half)

FLIGHTLESS CORMORANT
Has lost the ability to fly, but is good at swimming

SEA LIONS
Approximately 50,000 of them!

MARINE IGUANAS
The only lizards that swim in the ocean

SALEMA FISH
Swim in large schools

Yellowtail Surgeonfish

King Angelfish

Sergeant Major

FISH
Over 50 species of fish found nowhere else in the world

WHALE SHARKS
A large mouth for feeding on plankton

Rainbow Wrasse →

AMAZON RAINFOREST

Traversing 9 countries, the Amazon is the largest and most biodiverse area of tropical rainforest on the planet

FROGS

Glass frog

Blue poison dart frog

Poison dart frog

Surinam horned frog

BIRDS

Chestnut-fronted macaw

Spectacled owl

Amazon kingfisher

Blue-and-yellow macaw

Hyacinth macaw

Crimson topaz

Oropendola

Scarlet macaw

Scale-crested pygmy tyrant

Capped heron

King vulture

Blue-fronted amazon

Yellow-headed caracara

SLOTHS
Very. Slow. Movers.

GREEN ANACONDA
Up to 5 metres long

Wire-tailed manakin

Grey-winged trumpeter

Swallow-tailed hummingbird

Plum-throated cotinga

Masked trogon

CAPYBARAS
A large semi-aquatic rodent

BLACK CAIMANS

AMAZON RIVER DOLPHINS
Also known as Pink Dolphins

RED-BELLIED PIRANHAS
Very sharp teeth!

BASILISK LIZARD
(a.k.a. Jesus lizard)

Can walk on water!

ELECTRIC EELS
Shock their prey with 600 volts of electricity

TREES
16,000 different species of trees

TOUCANS
Regulate body temperature with their beaks

KINKAJOU
Can turn its feet backwards and run in the opposite direction

MONKEYS

Spider monkey

Emperor tamarin

Capuchin monkey

Squirrel monkey

Marmoset

Rubber tree (*Hevea brasiliensis*, Sap used to make rubber)

Huasai tree / palmito (*Euterpe precatoria*)

Barrigona, pona or huacrapona (*Iriartea deltoidea*)

Huicungo (*Astrocaryum murumuru*)

Palla, conta or shapaja (*Attalea butyracea*)

JAGUAR
The third largest cat in the world

Walking palm / cashapona (*Socratea exorrhiza*)

Kapok tree (*Ceiba pentandra*) Grows up to 70 metres high

ARAPAIMA
The Amazon's biggest fish

GIANT ANTEATERS
60cm-long tongue

← Grows up to 3 metres →

GIANT OTTER

THE AMAZON RIVER
The second longest river in the world

RIO DE JANEIRO

A city surrounded by mountains and beaches, with a non-stop carnival atmosphere!

← **CHRIST THE REDEEMER STATUE**
30 metres tall and a lot bigger than this drawing

COATI
Lives in large social groups of up to 30 individuals

TIJUCA FOREST
The largest urban forest in the world ↓

SUGARLOAF MOUNTAIN
396 metres high

BOTECOS
A great place to enjoy a refreshing drink

RIO CARNIVAL
An annual festival filled with dancers, floats and more than 200 samba schools

Don't forget your suncream! ↓

BEACHES
Over 50km of beautiful beaches

CAPOEIRA
A Brazilian martial art that combines dance, music and acrobatics

On the beach

In nappies

On the
streets

FOOTBALL
A national pastime played
by everyone, everywhere!

With a
walking
frame

On the pitch

Watching
television

On the move

**MURALS, MOSAICS
AND STREET ART**
On many walls
around the city

FAVELAS
A city within a city,
around 20% of Rio's
6.3 million people live in
these makeshift towns

MARACANÃ STADIUM
Holds the world record for
stadium attendance (199,854 people)

The Favela
Painting Project

Mural
Babilonia

Selarón Steps
Over 2000 tiles
from over 60
countries

Women
Are
Heroes
paste-
up

Cape Town

One of South Africa's three capital cities, a place of natural beauty with a diverse cultural history

TABLE MOUNTAIN
Approximately 5.1 million years old →

PORT OF CAPE TOWN
One of the busiest shipping corridors in the world

Get your swank on! →

ARCHITECTURE
Dutch, French, German, Victorian, and Malay influenced buildings

SWANKERS/SWENKAS
Well-dressed gentlemen competing to look the sharpest and swankiest!

Martin Melck House
One of the oldest colonial homes in South Africa

Houses of Parliament
Built in 1884

Bo-kaap ↑
Colourful homes built by Muslims from East Africa and South East Asia

Green Point Lighthouse
The oldest operational lighthouse in South Africa

Castle of Good Hope
The oldest building in South Africa
(built 1666–1679)

City Hall
Built in 1905

WHALES
Watch for migrating whales from July to November

BEACH CABINS
Colourful changing cabins (a.k.a Umkleidekabine) at Muizenberg beach

BUTTERFLIES
Aeropetes tulbaghia a.k.a.
Table Mountain Beauty

ORCHIDS
Disa uniflora a.k.a.
The Pride of Table Mountain

CREATURES BIG AND SMALL
The Big Five
and
the Little Five

Lock your
windows!

African bush elephant

Cape elephant shrew

CHACMA BABOONS
Very intelligent and always
looking for an easy meal!

Rhinoceros

Rhinoceros beetle

Buffalo

Red-billed
buffalo weaver

Lion

Antlion

Leopard

Leopard tortoise

GREATER FLAMINGOS
Get their pink colour from
pigments in the food they eat

SURFING
Lots of beaches,
lots of waves